Discipline, Boys, and School Problems

What's Wrong with the "Get Tough" Policy?

An excerpt from *Teenagers and Parents: 12 Steps to a Better Relationship*

Dr. Roger McIntire

Summit Crossroads Press
Columbia, MD.

Copyright 2016 by Roger W. McIntire

This is an excerpt from *Teenagers & Parents: 12 Steps for a Better Relationship* by Dr. Roger McIntire. The complete book may be ordered from Amazon.com, other online bookstores and wherever books are sold.

Teenagers & Parents: 12 Steps for a Better Relationship is approved by Parents' Choice Foundation.

Orders of 10 or more copies are available for a considerable discount from the publisher.

Published by Summit Crossroads Press, Columbia, MD, USA. Contact: sumcross@aol.com or 410-290-7058.

ISBN: 978-0-9614519-7-4

All rights reserved. No part of the material protected by this copyright notice may be reproduced or utilized in any form or by any means, electronic or mechanical, including photocopying, recording, or by information storage and retrieval systems without written permission from the publisher. Printed in the United States of America.

Dr. Roger McIntire is available for speaking engagements. His books provide excellent discussion material for parenting groups. E-mail: sumcross@aol.com.

Table of Contents

What's Wrong with the "Get Tough" Policy? - 9
1. Ten Reasons Advice From "Get Tough" Uncle Harry Is Off Track - 10
2. Negative reinforcement - 26
3. Why Would Anyone Use Punishment? - 35
4. Five Alternatives to Punishment - 36
5. Use a Behavior Checklist in Your Planning Session - 58

Help with the "Boy Problem" and School Work - 65
1. The "Boy Problem" - 65
2. Who is Gifted? - 70
3. Bullies and Victims - 77
4. Magical Thinking and Mental Habits - 84
5. Providing Answers to, *Why Should I Do That Stuff?* - 93
6. Homework Strategies That Work - 99
7. How About a Computer Program to Help Learning? - 110
8. An Additional Schoolroom Strategy - 112

4 - Dr. Roger McIntire

Preface

All of the theories—about siblings, birth order, genetics, and early experiences—contribute understanding, but such past influences cannot be changed. Mom's and Dad's best opportunity to influence their teenager, really their only opportunity, is confined to the here-and-now—the present family interactions.

Boys are five times more likely than girls to have accidents with bikes, sticks and baseball bats. Later on, they are four times more likely to have trouble with the law. In the U. S., boys cause most teen driving accidents and get most of the traffic tickets. They also have lower grades in school and are more likely to drop out. Boys have shrunk to a minority in colleges, medical schools, and law schools. Although girls were rarely even allowed in these institutions a century ago, now, for every 100 male college graduates there are over 140 women graduates. The genders are different and there is a "Boy Problem."

Many counselors believe that parents who hold back too much have a lasting negative influence on their children. One counselor friend of mine works with corporate administrators who often suffer from depression. She said she often found that the root of the problem was an unfulfilled need for acceptance from their Dads. She added that every man longs for the day when his father says, "You're the son I hoped you would be."

Daughters have had the same longings, I'm sure, and Mom's acceptance is just as important as Dad's. But Dads may hold back on the gushier stuff just when it's needed most. Often called upon to be the heavies— Wait 'till your father gets home!—Dads may miss their opportunities to give deserved praise and admiration.

The struggle to grow up is a confusion of emotions mixed with a desire to break free from parental control and a desire for parental admiration and support. Of course, teenagers want to be on their own and different from their parents. And conversely, parents want their children to stay close to their example and be more like them. The compromise develops gradually in a mixture of granting greater independence and decreasing control.

What's Wrong with the "Get Tough" Policy?

Punishment is a tempting strategy when bad behavior demands immediate reaction, and the long-term relationship with your teen is temporarily less important. But punishment doesn't deliver the needed information about what a teen needs *to do*. You can't make a garden just by pulling weeds; you have to grow something, plant something.

The family needs to be a place where training through trial-and-error is encouraged and guided. This is the opposite of what is created when punishment is used.

"You're too easy on the kids! Let me have them for a week. They'll shape up after a couple of swats from their Uncle Harry!" Nancy and Martin are a sister and brother team who started their game when they were five. Now in their teens, they know all the buttons to push to get

the reactions they want. They're still playing their game of *"Let's-see-how-much-we-can-get-away-with."* They either conspire to work their parents up or they bug each other and get parent attention as a bonus. Any suggestion to Nancy or Martin by their parents that they do *"something useful"* is rejected, perhaps because that would mean the game would be over.

1. Ten Reasons Advice from "Get Tough" Uncle Harry is Off Track.

Most of the relatives, including Uncle Harry, think they could fix the Nancy-and-Martin problem with stern talk and extra punishments—restrictions or removed privileges. Uncle Harry thinks he would somehow use punishment more effectively and more consistently than Nancy's and Martin's parents.

Reason #1: Uncle Harry's Hard-Line Approach Will Be, Must Be, Inconsistent.

The first problem with Uncle Harry's use of the straight punishment rule is that even Uncle Harry cannot, *and should not*, be consistent with it. Punishment would be too inhuman without the inconsistencies of warnings and threats.

If Uncle Harry's reactions could be as consistent and as quick as, say, an electric shock from a wall outlet, he might make some short-term progress.

Wall outlets and lamp sockets will consistently punish us without warning; they don't hesitate because we look cute trying to be "devilish." They don't think we've had a bad day or haven't been reminded lately of what will happen if we mishandle them. We get none of this consideration, and we are careful not to mistreat outlets and lamp sockets.

But Uncle Harry is not a wall outlet. Out of love and sympathy neither Mom, Dad, nor Uncle Harry can resist preceding punishments with the warnings and threats and so the game begins. When the kids were younger, spankings might have been used. But you can't spank the big ones and anyway, even spanking would have to include lots of warnings.

Parental consistency is always desirable and basic to learning. The lack of consistent reactions, on the reward side, leads to confusion and slows the pace of progress. The inevitable inconsistency of punishment brings on additional problems. Remember that "mean" teacher you had in school? Mr. Meany, or maybe it was a Ms. Meany, used punishments, reprimands, sarcastic remarks, put-downs, and embarrassments whenever the kids deviated from the desirable, and sometimes even when it seemed the kids had done nothing wrong! I bet you hated that class!

A student's greatest fear is to be embarrassed. With "Mr. Meany," you just couldn't be sure when you might trigger an embarrassing reaction. *All* behaviors (even volunteering right answers, suggestions, or questions) were reduced because you and your friends just wouldn't risk it. Not surprisingly, most "mean" teachers think the students in their classes are not very smart.

When punishment is uncertain, students become very cautious, especially when they are around the teacher who punishes. Around other people, bad behavior may increase to let off the oppressed steam or just to somehow even the score for the whole day.

Parents also can fall into the "mean teacher" trap,

and their kids may learn to behave whenever Mom threatens them or looks mad. As Mom realizes this works, she may increase "looking (and acting) mad" to include most family moments. Parents in this pitfall soon find that "looking mad" won't do, and they have to act "really mad." Now Dad and Mom have been pushed up a notch toward becoming behavior problems themselves!

So for Nancy and Martin to grow into happy, independent, productive adults, they need alternative activities that make the *"Let's-see-what-we-can-get-away-with"* game unimportant. Mom and Dad need to catch opportunities to encourage the kids. They also need to sharply limit punishment and use alternatives such as allowing the kids to make amends for mistakes as we do adults.

Carrying out all of this is more difficult and requires more planning than hard-headed Uncle Harry's idea of *"thrashing it out of them."*

Reason #2: The Punishment Trigger is a Parent's Exasperation, Not a Teen's Behavior.

In most parenting situations, punishment is a dangerous practice partly because it may be more related to the frustrations and moods of a parent than to a teenager's mistakes. Frequent use of punishment, when Dad or Mom have had it "up to here," usually results in a teen more interested in the moment-to-moment mood of his parents than his own rights and wrongs.

So Martin and his sister become manipulators who know that as long as they don't push too far, they're safe. They can predict punishment better, but still not perfectly, by watching their parents' emotions rather than adjusting their own behavior.

So Uncle Harry's punishment is inconsistent because it will be related more to his frustrations and moods than to the mistakes of the kids. If Dad or Mom use Harry's idea when they have had it "up to here," Nancy and Martin will only be interested in that frustration point as their signal to ease up just short of the boiling points of Mom and Dad.

Reason #3: Punishment will be Imitated.

We usually think of a teen's imitation of parents as very specific. *"Look at the way he walks, just like his Dad." "Look at the way she does her hair, trying to be just like Mom."* But copying Mom and Dad is more likely to involve social habits. How does Mom handle situations when things don't go right? What is Dad's solution when others don't do what he wants? If Dad gets frustrated, how does he react?

We all know how quickly kids will pick up those words of frustration when Dad hits himself on the kitchen drawer, but they also pick up the cues on *how to react* when things go wrong. Kids may get the message that the punishments used by Mom and Dad are good ways to deal with people.

The imitation of punishment will be included in the rest of your teen's social life. How should he handle friends when they don't do the "right thing?" A parent becomes a role model for punishment. *"It works for Mom, maybe it will work for me when I feel like it."* In any case, the most natural reflex to punishment is to give some back.

If it is not possible to punish his parent, your teen

might turn to others.

So there's the possibility that your teen will pick up some cues from your behavior about what is the appropriate reaction to unwanted behavior. If your daughter frequently criticizes and yells at her baby brother, a careful observation of her parents' own reactions might discover a clue as to where a daughter's reactions come from.

Teenagers make a lot of mistakes, being led into errors by peers, forgetting chores and commitments, indulging in unhealthy foods, and wasting time, to mention a few. When parents see so many errors, they may find it difficult to be accepting and look at the long run. But the goal of teaching how to react to others may be more important than correcting the mistake itself.

Reason #4: Punishment is Insulting, Belittling, and Lowers a Person's Self-Esteem

The emotional put-down of punishment distracts the victim from learning about the desired behavior. The punishment act, itself, is childish and belittles the significance of the victim. Isn't that why *adults* are so insulted when punishment is tried on them? So we all learn that the only possible ages for punishment are from 2 to 18. Before that, it's called abuse; After that, it's hopeless.

Once a teen's value of himself goes down and the fear goes up, a new disadvantage develops for learning. Much of the teenage years are a trial-and-error process. The discoveries of "how to get along" come from a lot of guesses. How much guessing will a frightened person risk? Once your teen becomes discouraged and engaged in self-degrading thoughts, parents and teachers know learning will be slow.

In my college course in animal learning, students had to teach their own pigeon to perform tasks by rewarding small successes. The first task was to get the pigeon to peck a disc by rewarding it with seeds, first for stepping toward the disc, followed by putting its head toward it, then touching it, and finally pecking it.

Sometimes students had trouble with the project because their pigeon was too scared to even move in its cage. If it had been handled roughly or it had escaped and been chased down before being put in the learning cage, it was too upset to do anything! Pigeons that won't do anything can't be taught anything! The student stared at the pigeon waiting for a chance to reward success. The pigeon stared at the student waiting for a chance to get out!

Punishment can produce the same impasse between teen and parent.

Reason #5: Punishment Encourages Stressful Behaviors.

Punishment will encourage bad habits such as nail-biting, hair-twirling, and *"safer obsessions"* like video games and TV. These *"escapes"* are very stubborn habits maintained by their usefulness for avoiding contact with the punisher. Whenever encouragement and reward are low, these stress behaviors will increase. If the stressful behavior attracts some parental attention, then we are in a vicious cycle with a new long-term problem.

Reason #6: The Power Struggle.

Punishment will tempt your teen to resist his parent's intimidation; the struggle takes over the family airways leaving little time for positive interactions and learning. A parent can "win" the power struggle, but, again, for every winner a loser is made!

The power struggle of punishment can spread to all family members. As others pick up the habit, a competition develops, *"Who can 'outdo'* (put down, criticize, reprimand, catch more mistakes of) *whom?"* It ruins the family as a nurturing place where learning is encouraged through practice—*with* mistakes.

Reason #7: Punishment is a Short-term Trap That Can Last Forever!

The *parental* bad habit of using punishment can be stubborn because it produces short-term results. For example, when Martin aggravates his Aunt Hazel, she may keep him in line by finding fault where he is vulnerable, *"That music is terrible. Your hair is a mess! Your face is breaking out again."*

With each of these insults, Martin's obnoxious behavior is temporarily interrupted while he defends himself, Aunt Hazel has released a little tension, and maybe Hazel has "taught Martin a lesson" or at least evened the score.

The long-term disadvantages of Hazel's punishment habit may go undetected because they will grow slowly. Martin will start the bad escape habits, he will feel worse about himself and about Aunt Hazel, and *he* will try to use punishment himself.

These two people are well on the way to a poor relationship where Martin annoys Aunt Hazel just to get even and Aunt Hazel boils over now and then to gain temporary relief from her allergic reaction to him. Martin will learn when to let up a little, and he may also learn to imitate her insulting style just to gain more control.

Reason #8:   Discrimination.

A teen subjected to a parent or relative in the *"I'll-get-even-with-you"* game learns the signals well. Innocent chaperones and teachers become fair game until they learn how to insult or scowl miserably enough to get control. An additional social problem is that no adult around a teen like Martin likes to be forced to act mad or abusive and would rather avoid him, partly because they don't like the person they must become to keep control.

Parents suffer the most from the frequent punishment policy, and their teens may suffer less because they learn to adjust to people who will play their game and those who will not.

We all develop discriminations and act differently with different people. But when punishment is used, we do our best to avoid the punishing person altogether. The negative, critical and threatening boss may have a reputation as a hard-liner, but the employees will duck and dodge her as much as possible. And they'll give no extra effort. Who wants to please her?

The relationship that develops is one in which two people only barely tolerate each other because they are forced to. A teen may like to escape such a situation because of the possibility of being punished, and a parent may want to be away (at work, at meetings, or just out anywhere) because of the uncomfortable parental reactions that seem to be called for in the situation.

Reason #9: Relatives Will Go Home, Parents Will Be Left Behind.

When Uncle Harry leaves, Mom and Dad are left with the long-term side effects of punishments that were too severe and too frequent. Your teen's solution may be to stop responding altogether or, at least, to respond as little as possible. The situation has produced a kind of success, your teen *is* quiet.

Even if the adults try a better approach later on, Nancy and Martin may refuse to risk coming out of their shells. The biggest wish of these kids is to get out—out of the room, out of sight, out of the house, if possible. Wouldn't we all rather dodge the punishment? With punishment you have to find your teen; with praise, your teen finds you.

With repeated experience, the situation preceding punishment signals a need to withdraw. The signal could be a classroom, a house, a time of day, a particularly dangerous person, or a combination of these. Once experiences have taught these signals, the mere termination of punishment is not likely to be effective immediately, because a teen in these circumstances will be unwilling to take risks to find out if danger has passed.

Uncle Harry and Aunt Hazel will leave behind other unintended effects. Activities and behaviors that explore new opportunities for learning may be reduced because they now seem dangerous or potentially embarrassing. Often an uncle's opinion of your son or daughter is better understood than the specific reasons for punishment. The details of why he was so angry are smothered in the emotion, fear, and desire to suppress the memory of the whole experience. The lack of understanding combines with the fear of risking any more punishment, and we are well on the way to stopping all progress in this situation.

Left on their own with Harry's punishment advice, parents will be tempted to increase punishment when the kids don't seem to get the message. But punishment gives too little information—it only tells you one of the things you ought *not* to do, nothing about what *to do*.

To reverse Uncle Harry's effects, a reduction in punishment must be accompanied with an increase in opportunities for genuine encouragement. Very minor events can act as punishments for a timid teen. Simply interrupting him at dinner may silence him for the whole meal. A verbal snap from his sibling may accomplish the same thing. It will require many isolated one-on-one moments with generous parents showing great tolerance and support to draw him out.

Many of Uncle Harry's threats will very likely be of the one-shot nature if his stay is longer than a week (perish the thought). As the punishments fail to produce results, he may opt for larger punishments such as canceling a trip or party. Usually one-shots are too late and produce the most resentment and argument with the least amount of change. Since parties and trips are infrequent, Uncle Harry feels he has to threaten a lot just to milk as much influence as possible from the upcoming event. Once the party or trip is over, a new threat will have to be dreamed up, or, if Harry's gone, the parents will be left with that job.

The one-shot leaves parents with the dreary task of sorting out threats, bluffs, and final conclusions. In the process they are likely to fall into a negative reinforcement habit (see below).

Reason # 10: Punishments Can Lead to Divorce.
Any person being punished has one thought in mind, *"Get away!"* Teens could plan running away or withdrawing if running away is impractical. And yet the conflict and confusion are intensified because your home is their most important source of security.

So don't talk about divorcing your teenager. This ultimate consequence is too disturbing and implies that your love for your teen can be easily traded away. Your love and loyalty should have a higher price tag and should not become part of bluffing or bargaining.

Whenever punishment is used, we are counting on some other aspect of the situation to keep our teen within range for deserved punishments. Either the doors must be locked, literally or figuratively, or the rewards from parents are enough to overwhelm the unhappiness. No matter how effective punitive measures may seem in the short-run, parents risk losing their teen. One reason punishment strategies usually don't work on adults is that adults can leave.

2. Negative Reinforcement.

Isn't negative reinforcement the same as punishment? No, it's more subtle but also more common. The purpose of regular punishment, as everyone knows, is to reduce or eliminate bad behavior. Negative reinforcement is not punishment for mistakes, it's punishment for *failing* to do the right thing! The threat of a consequence for failing to meet someone's expectations is a common experience in a routine day.

Why do I make dinner for the kids at the same time every night, use their favorite plate, prepare only certain foods? Is it because they watch for their chance to support my "good" behavior? No, the answer here usually begins, *"Well, if I didn't do that, the kids would complain and make a lot of trouble."*

When it is the *lack* of performance that produces bad consequences, it's called negative reinforcement. As long as I avoid unwanted dinner plates, unwanted food, delays, and don't disappoint my little masters, *I avoid* their nasty behavior.

Parents also use negative reinforcement. For

example, as long as the kids don't act up or fight, *they can avoid* their parents' angry reaction.

The difference between regular punishment and negative reinforcement is important because the threat of negative reinforcement is always hounding the child-teen. It has a continuous nature to it and, if not tested, the fear can continue long after the threat has passed.

Punishment in its consistent form, even with all its faults, is easy to understand: *"If I do the wrong thing, I'll get bad consequences."* Negative reinforcement has all the same faults as punishment with the added confusion of an obscure rule: *"If I fail to do the right thing, I'll get bad consequences."*

> Mom: *"Zac, did you pick up your clothes?"*
> Zac: (Watching TV) *"Not yet."*
> Mom: *"Did you put your dirty clothes in the laundry?"*
> Zac: *"No."*
> Mom: *"How about the mess in the living room?"*
> Zac: *"OK, as soon as this is over."*
> Mom *"Take those dishes out, too."*
> Zac: *"OK"* (Remains an intimate part of the couch.)

> Mom: (She's used no punishment so far, but now she reacts to Zac's *lack* of action.) *"Zac, I have had it! Now turn off that TV and get these things cleaned up!"*
>
> Zac: *"OK, OK, don't have a cow about it."*
>
> (Mumbling) *"Gee, who knows when you're gonna blow up, anyway?"*
>
> Mom: *"What was that?"*
>
> Zac: *"Nothing."*

Part of Zac's and Mom's problem is that Mom's strategy is the use of negative reinforcement. If Zac fails to perform (enough times) and Mom asks him (enough times) then Mom gets mad. Mom may also support and compliment Zac if he cleans things up, but Mom's exasperation limit and Zac's fear of her are the main factors at work in this situation.

At times, the distinction between punishment and negative reinforcement may seem like a word game. Could we simply say that Mom threatens punishment for Zac's sloppiness? She could use that strategy—dock his allowance when he leaves his clothes all over, for example. But her reaction is negative reinforcement because it is triggered by the *lack* of behaviors and occurs at a non-specific time. Zac is tempted to continue to procrastinate, delay, and test the limits while Mom is driven to using "mad" as a motivator.

Negative reinforcement does not produce a happy situation. If you do most of your activities everyday just to avoid someone's flack, you're probably unhappy with him or her (all spouses know who I'm talking about). *Positive* reinforcement is needed for a good relationship.

> Dad: *"Did you take the car in today?"*
> Mom: *"Yes, it just needed a tune up."*
> Dad: *"Great, thanks for getting it done; that takes a lot off my mind."*

Dad used the positive reinforcement idea, but in the next minute he slips to negative reinforcement:

> Dad: *"Did you get the little dinners I wanted for lunches?"*
> Mom: *"Didn't go by the store after work."*
> Dad: *"Hey, how am I supposed to work all day without lunch?"*

(Here's a reprimand as negative reinforcement

for Mom's failure to do the right thing.)
Mom: (Borrowing from Zac) *"OK, OK, don't have a cow over it. I'll get them tomorrow and I'll make something good for you to take in the -morning."*
(Mumbling) *"Gee, beam me up, Scotty!"*
Dad: *"What was that?"*
Mom: *"Nothing."*

Children have a better chance finding positive reinforcements everyday because parents and teachers know kids have to be encouraged. But negative reinforcement is probably the more common experience for us all even if it is a less popular term. It occurs when a behavior is used to <u>avoid</u> a consequence: Make your bed or Mom will be mad. Do your homework or the teacher will embarrass you in front of the class. Be home on time or Dad will be furious. Even though the intentions in these examples are to motivate, they sound like—and they are—threats.

For a teenager, the situation requires an effort to avoid the threatened outcome. He might want to escape the situation altogether as with punishment and he could try to run away but usually he will try to deal with it.

Discipline, Boys, and School Problems - 31

We're all familiar with the dark cloud of negative reinforcement produced by past bosses or parents and the escape we, at times, wished for. We recognize it when we hear someone say, "Well, if I didn't do it, I'd get so much flak..." If your day is filled with such efforts to stay out of the line of fire, you probably have leaving on your mind.

If most of what your teen does is an effort to avoid punishment or embarrassment, he or she will find it hard to be happy but won't have the resources to leave.

A marriage held together by one spouse hopping from one task to another trying to keep the other spouse from getting mad is an example. This unhappy situation may last for years, and it doesn't make a pleasant home environment either.

Even with the threat removed, a teen (or spouse) may be afraid to risk ignoring an old threat actually removed long ago. It will take some time and courage to test the new situation.

So here's a possible resolution: Every day, find something to compliment, appreciate, and support.

Translate some old negative reinforcement into its flip side—the positive encouragement for what should be done instead of the criticism for failures. Gush a little, even if you have to be a little corny. Tell your teen you noticed when he makes a successful effort—cleaned up some dishes—said something nice to his brother—got ready for school without complaints about clothes and lunches.

This "behavioral smile" is contagious; the kids are likely to copy your effort and the new style will recycle through the family. Keep it up—even a spouse can pick up the habit!

Negative reinforcement in combination with an upcoming, one-shot event is a tempting strategy to try to get the kids to do right. *"If you don't stop complaining all the time, we'll just give up going to the beach this summer."* or, *"You had better show me you can get along with your brother or I won't sign you up for soccer this year."* Because the threatened events happen only once or, at most, once a year, they can't be a part of *repeated* practice—unless we add a lot of nagging, *"Remember what I said, treat your brother nice or no soccer!"*

The threats for not acting right sound a lot like negative reinforcement with all its bad baggage, so nagging sets in to try to use the future one-shot event to get a little cooperation now.

Also, going to the beach is a singular future event not likely to be repeated for some time. Mom and Dad may repeat the *threat* many times since the vacation itself will only happen once. Of course, your teen needs to learn that you mean what you say about the beach or about soccer, but the consequence is so far off that any outcome may seem arbitrary.

So after all the argument, you either take the kid to the beach anyway, or you hold to your threat and don't take her/him. The first choice seems too lenient, but the second is too tough because it says that overall, he/she has been a bad kid. This one-shot consequence has no winners and little chance of a satisfactory outcome.

This situation is gloomy for the family and for the event when it finally comes. It's like holding off the enemy in battle with only one bullet; you have to do a lot of posturing, bluffing, and threatening. Once you use your bullet, you are an ogre for not allowing the beach or soccer or you are a patsy for giving in! And then the next day, you will need to threaten with a new bullet.

A better strategy is to allow yourself and your family the enjoyment of individual events without trying to use them to limit bad behavior or produce good behavior. Instead, choose some smaller event that can come up more frequently, something not so severe, that has a positive side to emphasize. For example, instead of threatening to ground your teen next semester if grades don't come up (an unmanageable threat with an "only once" character to it), possibly each good grade on any test, quiz or paper could produce a guaranteed 2 weeks of regular "going out" curfew privileges. This procedure has the advantage of being a consistent and repeatable consequence while a parent emphasizes the right habits. It is not negative or severe, so parents don't need to feel guilty and inconsistent. Also, it is logically related to the need for study time.

A very repeatable consequence makes it much easier to refrain from nagging. The repetition does the reminding. Nagging on the problem can stop, and the airways can be opened up for more pleasant family talk.

3. So Why Would Anyone Use Punishment?

With all these discouraging problems, one might wonder why some parents continue to use punishment. Even the choice of punishment should diminish when it is unsuccessful. So when a parent's action (punishment) doesn't get the desired result, why don't they just quit?

The answer is that in the very short term, punishment produces some results. If Mom punishes Fred for using bad language by grounding him, Mom's punishment behavior is reinforced by its immediate effect of interrupting Fred's bad behavior even if only temporarily. So Mom is tempted to use it again.

Parents, particularly American parents, hurried by schedules filled with job and family responsibilities, often hope for the "quick-fix." Punishment may seem to fill the bill, but we seldom try it on adults. Instead, we use one of the following alternatives.

4. Five Alternatives to Punishment

A large investment firm reneged on an announced $1.3 million dollar profit a few years ago because an accountant left off the minus sign—it was really a $1.3 million dollar *shortfall!* How did the firm's president discipline his accountant for the $2.6 million dollar mistake? To his disappointed stockholders he said, *"Well I guess that's why they put erasers on pencils!"* With adults, we usually get on with fixing the mistake. We deal with unwanted adult behavior every day, but like the accountant's president, most of us gave up punishment of the straightforward kind long ago.

The culture we live in continues to provide some punishment—"logical consequences" we sometimes call them—and the courts hand out punishments for the larger transgressions. But logical consequences and court sentences are usually long delayed and given only for repeated bad habits and big mistakes. So with unwanted *adult* behavior what punishment alternatives do we use?

Every day, adult mistakes receive *very kind* reactions.

Even blowing your horn at a poor driver's mistake is considered too aggressive. Often we just allow the person to make amends, or we ignore the mistake altogether. If we control the situation, we might try to make it less likely that he will repeat the mistake: *"The boss should give better instructions. He should put up more signs about how to use the printer!"* After more instruction, the boss may use warnings: *"Anyone caught putting their sandwich in the printer will be ..."* Then, if that doesn't work, maybe, punishment. Since punishment has so many disadvantages anyway, let's get on to a more adult way of handling problems.

Alternative #1: Making Amends.

Making amends is the number one strategy adults use to handle bad adult behavior. If you come to my house for dinner tonight and spill your drink at the table, you don't expect me to threaten punishment by saying: *"Hey! What do you think you're doing? You're so clumsy! Now pay attention to what you're doing, or I'll send you home!"*

What nerve! Treating a guest like a child. What happened to "the benefit of the doubt?" You expect to be allowed to make amends; you expect me to belittle the problem, you even expect sympathy. *"Oh, too bad. No problem, I'll get a cloth."* You say, *"I'm sorry, let me get that. I'll take care of it."*

Isn't adulthood nice? Even with big mistakes, we would rather have the offender try to fix the mistake than punish him. At what age did you, and our innocent accountant with the 2.6 million dollar mistake, earn such consideration? Why wasn't *he* punished? Because it wouldn't help and it would look as if the investment firm was a simple-minded company, naive and heartless. After all, mistakes happen.

Two-year-olds, teenagers, and accountants who make mistakes, accidental or not, should be allowed to make amends. Not that our accountant could make up for his mistake in this century. Your teen deserves the same respect. It is only fair to assume he or she is doing his or her best.

Remember the movie about a troublesome city teenager whose life was popping with mistakes that he could never see coming? His parents punished him, hoping he would avoid future "accidents." At last, in exasperation they sent him to the country to live with relatives. We saw our teen toil the whole afternoon, making amends for a clumsy mistake, spilling the milk can, before supper—cleaning up the spill. Finally finished, he went into dinner, justified, un-criticized, and with an experience that motivated him to be more careful.

At home he would have been restricted or physically punished and belittled, and he would have lost practice at making things right. Though the movie lesson was unrealistically easy and quick, the message was a good one: our teen learned by making amends and cleared up his guilt; the adults maintained a healthier relationship with him in the bargain.

> Grandma: (Sitting down to dinner) *"Whoops, now I know what I forgot at the store—coffee! But we have juice, how about that?"*
> Mom: *"Don't worry about it; juice is fine. We'll get the coffee tomorrow."* (Mom belittles the mistake)
> Grandma: *"At least I'll get out the juice."* (Grandma makes amends)
> Nancy: *"I accidentally erased our list of names and

> *addresses from the computer today."*
>
> Grandma: *"What! Didn't you put it back from the flash drive? I was looking for that for half an hour this afternoon. You're so inconsiderate at times. Don't you have enough sense to..."*
>
> Mom: (Interrupting) *"Nancy, after dinner, find the right flash drive and reload the address file, OK?"* (And then to Grandma) *"I can get along without the coffee until tomorrow if you can, so don't worry about it."*
>
> Grandma: *"What? Oh, ah, yes, OK, OK. If I get a break on forgetting the coffee, I guess Nancy gets a break, too. And, Nancy, could you add the names on the outside of my phone book?"*

Alternative #2: Ignoring.

Ignoring behavior eventually decreases it, especially if our teen was acting up to get attention. If a parent can tough it out and hold back attention for bad language, our teen may go on to something else. The problem here is that in the short-run, *more bad behavior* is more likely rather than less. This bad behavior has been a part of a habit to get some entertainment or attention from Mom and Dad. Now his parents plan to cut that off. For example, no more attention for bad language.

If the usual amount of swearing will no longer work, what should our teen do? He may escalate the volume, frequency, or foulness of the talk. At the "higher" level, parents may break the new rule and punish this outrageous behavior. If that quiets things down, parents may return to the ignoring rule only to go back to punishment when the assault on the ears again reaches pain threshold. The process builds up a new level of bad behavior. Escalation is a very common problem because the natural childish ("teenish?") reaction to failure (to get attention) is escalation.

Ignoring means consistently overlooking relatively unimportant, undesirable behaviors and paying attention to other aspects of a teen's actions. When Tim shaved his hair nearly to the middle of his head, his parents felt it was within his personal grooming choices to do so, but when he slapped his younger sister, they reacted strongly. Their different reactions to these very different behaviors keep the priorities straight and reduce unnecessary criticism.

When you react to the behavior of your teen, keep the overall family atmosphere in mind. Sacrifice family atmosphere only when necessary. If an action has a low priority rating, it doesn't deserve your time and energy, nor a lot of family disruption.

You may want to ignore behaviors that occur only occasionally as well as others that come under your teen's growing sphere of control, for example: keeping a messy bedroom, using poor grammar, wearing strange outfits and unusual hairstyles. A parent's greatest influences on these daily habits will not be by way of arguments and consequences, but the model they present. Some behaviors are part of passing stages that will be outgrown, and therefore they are easier to ignore. When your teen invites a friend to visit, the bedroom will be spruced up to *their* level of tolerance. Unwanted grammar, language, clothing, and hairstyles are probably temporary, fluctuating with peer and media influences.

One 13-year-old, I know, sprayed her hair to stand up six inches above her forehead and wore glaring makeup, but she was a good student with pleasant social skills. It was a tribute to her parents' ability to overlook extremes of grooming and focus instead on her *important* actions. Extremes of personal care will probably change toward the norm when a teenager wants to fit into a different group or workplace.

Alternative #3: Adding Something Good to the Ignoring Plan.

Mom and Dad need to have a plan to encourage good behaviors and be alert to the first opportunity to work the plan! Ignoring the unwanted behavior *and* planning to encourage *specific, likely,* good behaviors will produce better results. The message needs to be clear: *"Now that's a good way to handle that." "I liked hearing about your report on the Civil War battle. You're learning about interesting things." "I noticed you helped clear the table after supper. That was great!"*

"Catch 'em being good" means recognize, praise, or reward the good behavior you see. Perhaps you remember as a teen thinking, *"When I make mistakes everyone notices and I get in trouble, but a lot of times I do well, and nobody says anything."*

To prevent unwanted behaviors, parents need

to "catch 'em being good," not just when the desired behavior occurs, but when a behavior in the right direction comes along. Actions that are improvements and a step forward need the most encouragement, recognition, praise, and reward.

Research tells us that catching people when they come near to appropriate behavior is a more efficient learning technique than punishment for errors. Considering all the possibilities for error, a teen isn't much closer to learning an important skill just by being told, *"Wrong!"*

Which choice is more likely to produce positive results?

> 1. Teen has no friends. You can:
> a. discuss the importance of having friends, or
> b. listen and encourage any socializing in the family and outside it.
> 2. This young adult pouts and sulks. Would you:
> a. tell him to stop being a sourpuss?
> b. ignore pouting and talk pleasantly when he is sociable?
> 3. He/she has no outside interests. You can:

> a. require your teen to choose two activities of his/her choice and insist on participation for a half-year, or
>
> b. you can be available to listen for his/her interests.

In the first example, discussing friendship will be pointedly painful to your teen, but listening and socializing in the family will provide practice and build confidence for your teen to reach out in other situations.

In example two, reactions of anger to pouting will give attention to poor behavior and possibly encourage it with an argument about its justification. The better plan is to support the less frequent, appropriate, pleasant interactions.

In the third case about outside interests, both choices are helpful for a teen who needs to develop activities. Insisting on some selections takes authority, but that may be an ingredient needed to get things started.

Alternative #4: Using the Cost of Inconvenience.

Many little inconveniences may seem trivial, at

first, but when put into practice they may be extremely effective. For example, if Dad has to put a penny in a jar on the kitchen table every time he loses his temper, it may seem like a trivial act for someone with plenty of pennies. But if the rule is strictly followed, the inconvenience of having to stop, get a penny, go into the kitchen and put it in the jar can be a very effective consequence. Pennies are unimportant but the behavioral "cost" makes this consequence work.

Many psychologists use the principle of inconvenience as a strategy for removing or reducing smoking in adults. The heavy smoker is instructed to keep an exact record of his smoking throughout each day. He carries a little notebook wherever he goes and writes down the time, to the minute, when he takes out a cigarette, and the time he puts it out. He may be asked to note the situation as well, including who was with him and what he was doing. Some psychologists also ask for the cigarette butts to be saved and brought in for counting. These tasks may not seem like consequences as we have discussed them so far, but they are consequences of a most useful type. They are costly in time and many a smoker is just too busy to make all those entries and save butts, so he takes a pass on having that cigarette.

Such a self-administered procedure requires a very cooperative and trustworthy subject. I have found the cost-of-inconvenience procedure useful when smokers referred to me have been told by their doctor that their health or even their life is at stake! They usually *want* the process to work, and they can be counted on to try hard. The procedure has not worked well when used on people who *"feel they should cut down"* or quit for the children's sake. With these less motivated subjects, it takes a stronger procedure than raising the cost of inconvenience.

Sometimes teenagers can be enthusiastic about a record-keeping procedure. One mother reported that her 19-year-old son, Damon, continually disrupted the family by "checking things." On some evenings, he insisted on checking as many as 70 things before going to bed. Damon checked to see if the back door was locked. He checked to see if the light was out in the basement. He checked to see if his pen was on his desk, and if his dresser drawers were completely closed. Some of this would have been reasonable, but the situation got out of hand when he checked the same thing for the fifth or sixth time in the same evening!

At first his checking was examined for the possibility that it was an attention-getting behavior. Some progress was made by reducing Damon's parents' attention to the excessive checking and increasing conversation time before he went off to bed. The most effective procedure was beginning a record of every item checked, the time it was checked, the result of the check, and what could have happened if the item had been left unchecked. The procedure involved so much writing and decision-making that it was nearly impossible to check 70 things each evening.

Because of the work and inconvenience of the procedure, Damon began to pass up items that were not so important, and he made a special effort to remember the ones already checked, or look at his record, so that he didn't have to do it again! The number of times Damon checked things soon was down to a level that was only a little unusual instead of disruptive to the family.

The same principle of inconvenience can be used to increase a habit. For example, good homework habits can be influenced by how convenient it is to get started. If there is a place to do homework with little distraction that is well supplied with paper and such, then we have a better chance of getting some homework done.

> Dianne: *"I'm not going to practice this stupid violin any more, it's too much trouble!"*
>
> Mom: *"Just another ten minutes, then you can quit."*
>
> Dianne: *"Phooey."*

Dianne's practice is best done in intervals that keep frustration to a minimum, but once Dianne begins, Mom hates to let her quit because it's such a hassle to get her to start again. Maybe Mom could do away with some inconveniences associated with Dianne's "restarts." She could help Dianne get out the music, set up the stand. Then while Dianne checks the tuning, Mom could turn off the TV and get everyone else far enough away. If some of the inconveniences could be done away with, maybe Dianne would practice more frequently.

> Mom: *"Let's set up a special place for you. How about*

> *in our bedroom? We're never in there when you need to practice and it's away from the TV and your brother. You can leave your music and stand out, and it won't be disturbed."*
>
> Dianne: *"OK, but I still think all this practice is stupid."*

We have not solved the violin problem by just finding a place for practice. Dianne is going to need more encouragement than that. Mom needs to visit the practice situation a lot, comment on Dianne's progress, and help the instructor find practice pieces that interest Dianne. But a place to practice easily, without frustrating start-up time, is a step toward making good practice convenient.

Alternative #5: Consequences, Even Time-outs, Must Give Way to Modeling.

Sometimes the bad behavior demands a reaction. We don't let adults get away with just anything and teens becoming adults shouldn't be misled that anything goes either. What alternative is there when bad behavior should not be ignored and making amends or hoping for opportunities for encouragement is not enough?

For young children, time-out is often a good solution but may not be appropriate for teens—especially older teens. We all know the drill of putting a child or teen on a chair or in his/her room for a little "cooling off" as a kind of punishment. The procedure can work well if the threats, arguments, and other verbal decorations that often precede the time-out can be kept to a minimum.

> Mom: (Liz throws a toy at her sister.) *"Liz! We don't throw toys. You could hurt someone. That's One!"* (Liz throws again.) *"Liz I told you, that's <u>Two</u>"*
> Liz: *"I don't <u>want</u> it!"* (Liz throws again.)
> Mom: *"OK, that's Three,"* Mom takes Liz to the kitchen chair and deposits her there.

Mom is doing well with her younger one. She doesn't talk much during the count which could lead Liz to act up more, she doesn't make a lot of threats, and she corrects the behavior in a way that can be used frequently—no dramatic punishment that requires a big build-up.

Time-out for young teens means spending a short

time in a quiet place, alone, after inappropriate behavior. It can be very successful. The separation of younger teens from others interrupts overheated verbal and physical reactions with a calming-down period. When your teen has regained emotional control, she or he can discuss what happened and plan changes. The time period that is most helpful is long enough to break up unwanted behavior and tempers, but short enough for everyone to remember clearly what happened and want to plan other reactions. Just having time-out for a minute or two is effective; a long time-out is not necessary, nor helpful.

This alternative cuts off fighting between siblings and helps a parent regain perspective and control, instead of escalating a problem situation. Parents who try time-out find it prevents them from using physical and verbal punishments they regret later.

When parents react with punishments, they frequently prevent discussion and planning for changes. Because of bad feelings, the bad behavior is likely to occur again. But after time-out, each person involved in the problem has a chance to tell his/her

Discipline, Boys, and School Problems - 53

feelings and make suggestions. A parent and teen can practice the listening and understanding, and gain experience planning for a change. Time-out sets the stage for a new beginning.

When Mom returned from shopping, she noticed lipstick on the kitchen wall. Mike had been talking on the phone instead of watching his younger sister, Tina, the wall artist.

> Mike: *"But I have to talk on the phone to my friends sometimes. It drives me crazy to watch Tina every minute. I shouldn't have to watch her this much! How could she do that? Mom, you've raised her all wrong. I'm not going to clean that up. I have to leave to go to the mall with Bill."*
>
> Mom: *"We're going to have to talk about this now."*
>
> Mike: *"I can't stand it! It's not my fault, and Tina should have to clean it up! Mom, you can't make me do this."*
>
> Mom: *"Mike, I'm getting mad and you're upset too. Cool off for five minutes in your room, and then we'll put our heads together to work this out."* (Mike stomps out to his room.)

When the two get together after cooling down,

it's more likely they will be able to make a compromise. Perhaps Mom, Mike, and Tina can do the wall cleaning together. The baby-sitting needs more planning and incentives. Mike needs some specific activities to do with Tina while baby-sitting, and he can be given extra time with his friends for doing a good job. When you try to reach a solution, if either you or your teen find you can't be reasonable, extend the time-out until all persons can contribute to the agreement.

Dad was proud of his intelligent daughters, but when the girls fought, he couldn't tolerate it. Joy and Bonnie started kidding around and then sparring in the upstairs hall. When a framed picture hit the floor, Dad ran to the stairway and shouted for them to stop, *"Joy and Bonnie, you go to your rooms and we'll discuss this in 15 minutes if you're ready to talk reasonably!"*

Dad's girls are almost adults; it's time for them to find ways to keep their playfulness from escalating to breaking up the house. Dad's discussion with them as near-equals may help them share responsibility for controlling themselves as they reach for adulthood.

For a teen who is almost an adult, the time-out

method will seem more and more childish. After all, except for long time outs in prisons, you seldom see it used in the adult world. Your example, on the other hand, will always be an influence to your teen even in the decades to come.

Both parent modeling and family identification help a young person keep direction. Mom said, *"In the Weiler family we try to think of and respect everyone in the family <u>and</u> outside of it. I expect you to live up to the Weiler standard."* Of course Mom's actions must follow her words. Family sayings get across things parents consider important. My father was fond of saying, *"With all thy getting, get understanding."*

The following examples I have heard show how modeling and positive consequences work together. A parent who wanted a teen to read books turned off the TV and began reading an exciting adventure novel aloud with her teen. A mother who wants her daughter to be honest can ask, *"Whose money is this under the kitchen table?"* instead of just pocketing it. When a father noticed shoes accumulating by the front door, he put his in the closet, and soon his teen's were not at the front door either. The power of what we do is surprising; it's natural for members of the family to observe and be affected by it. Imitation occurs every day.

A teen with whom I worked developed a problem controlling anger. He started fights when classmates teased him and felt bad about himself later. His parents needed to demonstrate and describe their methods of controlling anger in their lives. Mom shared a story: *"I was driving to the post office today and when I changed lanes, another driver honked a long time at me. I guess he thought I slowed him down. I felt mad and thought about pulling over and shaking my fist at him. But I said to myself, 'I'm angry, but I'm in control—not him. I'm not going to let him make me do something dangerous.'"* Sharing family experiences is an important part of modeling.

Try this modeling exercise. Bring family members together to make lists of each other's actions. Each person writes everyone's name, including his/her own, on a piece of paper. Ask each person to list the most positive action of each member of the family after each name. Which family members work hard? Which ones have the most interesting stories, are creative, dress fashionably, use good manners, tell jokes or funny stories? Add actions that come to mind, but keep them on the positive side. This is not a gripe session.

After everyone has written a list, exchange sheets and ask someone to tell one of the answers on the sheet. Talk over these answers briefly but move right along to the next person and answer. The idea is to have people think about the positive actions of the ones they live with and encourage these activities. If someone is getting too few items or items too unimportant, add some during the discussion to even the totals.

The last part of this exercise is a discussion in which people pretend they are other members of the family. Let people choose their roles, and everyone can guess who is pretending to be whom as the discussion goes along. Select a discussion topic such as, where should we go on the next family outing? The purpose is merely to see how alike we are and yet how we each have a different view of others. Also, we may gain a clearer understanding of how much of our personalities are a function of those we live with.

Allowing a teen to make amends, use time-outs, ignore some things, look for something good, or watch your own example, *all* require diligent effort. Contrary to the easy magical advice from aunts, uncles, or some professionals, being a parent can be downright hard work. So make sure you eliminate rules about trivial behaviors before you start any of these plans. Here's an exercise to start the habit of keeping the rules appropriate and on target.

5. Use a Behavior Checklist in Your Planning Sessions.

Planning sessions have a dangerous tendency to turn into general gripe sessions. Although complaining can be therapeutic for parents, they often jump around from one problem to another without concluding a plan for any particular problem.

So a planning session needs an agenda that will focus on effective parental reactions to a particular situation. The session should also produce an overall understanding of what is going on when the specific problem is encountered.

The purpose of the checklist is to do a complete

"walk through" of a problem. You may not always need such a complete analysis, but for the purpose of becoming alert to the possible aspects of behavior, this exercise will include all the steps.

First select a behavior that will be the problem under discussion in this session.

Create a checklist that shows specific behaviors, punishments, and alternatives you could use. As you create your checklist, think of the behavior you want. What would you have done if the wanted behavior had occurred instead of the unwanted action? Would you have reacted positively just as you reacted negatively to the error? Was any part of the desired behavior done before the mistakes were made? If so, what encouragement did you give? This list will be helpful when talking over a behavior with your teen. A sample list follows on the next page.

Fill out a behavior chart. A short outline of the chart is presented below. You will not yet have a record of the behavior as described in the last part of the chart, but you can put down your own observations as you remember them to answer those questions.

A Sample Behavior Chart

Fill in a chart, with the answers to these questions:

1: What is an objective description of the behavior problem?

2: What usually happened next?

3: Where would you place the possible blames and/or credits?

4: At what age would you expect an average teen to do what you are hoping will be done in this situation?

5: How could you allow more practice?

6: When do things happen? (Keep a record)

Review this check list for consequences as you consider possible reactions to the behavior. Pose each of the following questions in the planning session:

1. **Is the problem big enough to bother with?** Remember even a "No" here should indicate a strategy—a strategy to eliminate nagging yourself, or your teen, about the problem.

2. **Am I attempting too much at one time?** A tempting pitfall in parenting is to try too many

changes at once. Don't attempt to control eating, piano practicing, bed-making, and doing homework all at once. Concentrating on too many plans leads to mistakes and too much "policing." Think small. Begin with one rule at a time.

3. **Can the behavior be guaranteed without the management of consequences?** Some behaviors can be made impossible by engineering the environment and that strategy is sometimes easier than using rules. For example, keeping sharp knives in a high cabinet or assigning a special kitchen drawer of utensils for a son or daughter's cooking.

4. **Have we thought of all the consequences that could be maintaining the behavior?** A good way to separate consequences is to consider what we *have now*? What usually happens when the "bad" behavior occurs and what happens next? What usually happens if she performs correctly? If we select a new consequence, how should we set up *the practice*?

5. **Is the consequence a one-shot?** In the one-shot consequence, a rule that can only work once, a parent uses a promise of something good or threat of

something bad in the *future* as a consequence for a *present* behavior problem. Whichever way the consequence is stated, threat or promise, it has the same disagreeable characteristics: it is not repeatable, it tempts parents to use repeated threats and will probably be somewhat arbitrary in the end. And then the next day what shall we do? Start a new threat?

6. **Is the consequence too severe?** Be sure that your selection of a consequence is not a reaction to one case of bad behavior. You want something that can be used repeatedly. As a matter of fact, the real test will come after things have settled down. The main feature of your plan that will help you will be that you have planned to reward good behaviors reasonably and react to bad ones reasonably. So don't make plans when you're still angry over a mistake.

7. **If ignoring is the plan, are we prepared to handle the resulting escalation of the bad behavior?** And what good behavior will we be on the lookout for, give attention to?

8. **Is the expectation reasonable?** Your expectation may be reasonable but still much more

than your daughter has ordinarily been doing. She was cleaning her room and now you want her to vacuum and dust the house. Remember we need to start where *she* is, not where you *wish* her to be.

9. **Is the consequence too weak?** What can be done if your teen just doesn't seem to care about the new consequence? It could be that you are not sticking to the rule and he really doesn't *have* to care. Or possibly he has too many freebies available or too many alternatives (If I can't go out, I'll watch TV!).

Are you starting with a behavior simple enough so that rewards can occur—even on the first day?

10. Review this Check List for Alternatives to Punishment.

1. Could you use the adult reaction to adult mistakes, *making amends?*

2. Is it possible to first try *ignoring?*

3. Could we help him or her to see us as a *good model.*

4. Have the other possibilities presented in this been considered: *"Catch 'em being good,"* Changing *the convenience* of the behavior, and *"Time-outs."*

64 - Dr. Roger McIntire

Help with the "Boy Problem" and School Work

1. The "Boy Problem."

Of course, both girls and boys have problems. But, as a group, boys have more problems with social media and many other things.

The Southern Regional Education Board in 2012 studied 40,000 typical high school students, not stars and not low performers. While 84 percent of girls said it was important to continue schooling after high school, only 67 percent of boys agreed.

By 12th grade, 44 percent of girls have become proficient readers but only 28 percent of boys have reached that standard. Only 41 percent of boys said they "often" tried to do their best work in school, compared with 67 percent of the girls.

Now that the "male chores" of the farms of 1900

have become less needed, girls have an advantage. Girls make an earlier contribution to the family, particularly in the domestic chores. As a result, they enjoy early appreciation and are better prepared to care for themselves.

Parents tend to cave in to flack from boys while resisting any flack from girls. Insistence on girls doing their chores and homework, their skills develop as does their enthusiasm for work done successfully. Boys may receive less encouragement from exasperated parents or because boys dodge the work altogether, and they fall further behind in the experience department.

Dads are particularly vulnerable to competition with their sons and hold back on compliments for chores well done for fear of appearing weak.

Support your school's active projects in home improvement, financial management, small business management, mortgages, stock markets, computer management, applied science, and tracking diet and exercise. These projects encourage both boys and girls to be proud of their abilities right now. Even abstract subjects can include practical applications.

College applications may not ask about these "non-academic" skills, but schoolwork should help your son or daughter with concerns now, at their present age. "Someday you'll need this," is not enough. They need a good answer to, "What good is this (homework, project, learning, work) now?"

One source of the gender difference may come from the trend to single-parent families. The year 2000 U.S. Census said one-third of our children were raised in single-parent households, up from only one in 10 in 1960. These children were five times more likely to be raised by single Moms than single Dads. Girls will have a same-sex role model while the boys may be looking to teachers, relatives, and media for guidance part of the time. Whatever the sources of influence, the differences between boys and girls in school are worrisome.

Going from father to grandfather, I went from girls who have the highest grades in school and are the least likely to need school discipline, to boys who are most likely to be disciplined and six times more likely to have trouble with the law, with driving, with alcohol and drugs, and six times more likely to go to prison later on.

Is all this genetic? Some of it must be but there are positive, and negative, contributing factors from parents and grandparents.

Many parents, teachers, and counselors believe girls are more socially skilled at an earlier age and therefore may attract more support, acceptance, and admiration than their brothers. Boys on the other hand, seem to want only to be competent and be admired for it. They seem to shun the gushier praise.

Parents shouldn't be misled by a son's bland reaction. To prove they are not easily influenced, boys often fend off sincere praise in the years when they need it most.

The lack of enthusiasm from a son may lead parents to conclude that compliments and admiration don't work so they should lay off the positive approach. This is a deadly mistake.

Parents should not be misled by short-term rebuffs because the long-term results are more important. The temptation to let boys go their own way, with discipline for only the big blunders and a trickle of support for the successes, is destructive to skill development in boys.

Dads are particularly vulnerable to taking up this strategy and come off looking as if they never completely approve of anything their son does.

A strange effect of sexism in our culture is that girls sometimes show better adjustment in childhood than boys possibly because they make an earlier contribution to the family, particularly in domestic chores. They enjoy early appreciation and are encouraged to do more.

While "protecting" a boy from drudgery, parents can run the risk of driving their son to find other activities that show he can "do something."

Threatened by his perceived "worthlessness," he will cast around for a way to show off—what will he find? Will it be a suggestion from his Mom or Dad? Or will encouragement from friends make risky behaviors more likely?

Positive support is the major advantage parents have in competing against their teen's friends who encourage and criticize without much thought. Parents have to hold to limits that are not always popular, but also must inspire new tasks that build self-respect.

One fast way to alienate a member from a group (or family) is to deny him a chance to contribute when he's ready. Gripe as a son may about chore assignments and household jobs, recognition of his step forward now will help maintain his genuine satisfaction with himself later on when peers encourage dangerous habits.

Practical and active projects can inspire a teenager. Projects in home improvement, cooking, financial management, small business management, mortgages, stock markets, setting up a new cell phone and tracking diet and exercise all encourage boys as well as girls to be proud of their abilities right now. Even abstract subjects can include practical projects.

2. Who is Gifted?

Soccer and basketball coaches are not the only adults putting kids to the test and seeking the stars. The schools are forever testing our teens, looking for the "gifted." They do it because they have special programs for special kids. And some of us want "trophy children." But how would a parent recognize, and how should a parent react to, their teenager's "gifts?"

Who were the geniuses of the past? Einstein, for sure, even though his genius wasn't detected until he was nearly an adult. Many people would include Mozart who was writing operas at the age of three. But neither the musical genius of Mozart or Michael Jackson guaranteed a long and happy life.

We might include others in math and theoretical physics, as well as additional nominations from the list of classical composers. No doubt these people were born with something special. Einstein even left his brain to science so they could try to figure out what it was—they have offered no conclusions.

Schools usually limit definitions of "gifted" to areas they teach and evaluate—math, science, language-related talents such as those seen in spelling bee winners, and sometimes music.

Other gifts, such as social skills, artistic ability, and common sense, are not so easily evaluated. It may even seem silly and arbitrary to think of the "County Common Sense Champion" or the "Personality State Champion." But these other talents need to be recognized so that a parent's expectations can keep pace. Business professionals tell us that the strengths which lead to success are likely to be perseverance, hard work and social skills—not academic trophies.

I know a fifth grader who represented his county grade school at the national spelling bee in Washington D.C. We don't know if his spelling talents mean he could learn other languages at an astounding rate, but we know that multi-lingual applicants will be prized by businesses of the future. If we wait too long to teach languages to him, he will not be able to learn another language without an accent.

Is it enough to be proud of his accomplishment and continue his schooling with no foreign language training until high school? Should we take the wide view of "gifted" and let him at least sample challenging language training now? How many seeds of unrecognized genius wither because they did not fall on fertile ground?

Parents are often aggravated by their talented teenager's failure to carry through and use unusual blessings. Why would he come up short on effort when he has the gift? The answer, sometimes, may be that procrastination has set in because of fear of failure, particularly if failure is defined by himself or his parents as anything less than perfect.

One Mom told me her son brought home a poor report card. When she looked through his backpack she found completed history assignments, weeks after they were due. What's going on? Her son said his work was "not quite right." So he's a gifted perfectionist who is flunking history.

Keep a modest reaction if a coach or teacher says your teenager is gifted. If he turns into a perfectionist, he may avoid the risks of trying new activities and expressing new ideas. Don't be misled by society's narrow views of gifts and talent. Look for and encourage all your son's or daughter's gifts.

Concerning the lighter side of early development, take Alex, now 16. He spent his babyhood thumbing through magazines while his fellow one-year-olds played with simple toys. By the time he was three, he would correct his mother if she skipped reading a line in a story by placing her finger on the missed phrase.

Alex has *hyperlexia*, a condition opposite, in many ways, to the learning disorder, dyslexia. He has a very advanced ability to identify individual sounds while reading, and he also has an advanced ability to manipulate those sounds in his head. Nevertheless, he had trouble understanding what he read and he was delayed in learning to speak.

He now speaks in a normal fashion but uses the cadence of reading out loud, and he avoids interjections such as "like" that many youngsters his age use incessantly.

But Alex is running for his student council and he may win because he is a fearless public speaker. Alex seems about normal in any category outside of his language ability.

Helpful parents deserve daily credit for encouraging all competencies beyond what a scientific test might discover. They can help in all cases by watching for chances to bolster confidence and by avoiding the straight diet of advice, quick fixes, and focus on shortcomings that hit vulnerable spots.

"Practice what you want to become" is a good rule

for teenagers. "Model what you want your children to practice" is a good rule for parents.

How can you know which kids will get into trouble? The nightly news might give you the impression that low income and poor family structure are the primary causes of dangerous and destructive paths.

But the long-term Adolescent Health Study shows that the kids most likely to get into self-destructive activities such as drinking, drugs, or crime are kids who do poorly in school.

The study has been following 12,000 students since 1994 when they were 12 to 17 years old. It found all the familiar problems you would expect. At first, one in ten reported weekly drinking, and the amount of sexual behavior was alarming. One in five seventh and eighth graders had explored sexual activities, and two out of three high school juniors and seniors were sexually experienced.

After problems with school, the second best predictor of these bad habits was the amount of unsupervised time each teenager ordinarily had. This influence showed up in drug use, violent behavior, and sex. "Among all the factors that can be associated with teenage sex, the big one was opportunity," Dr. Robert Blum, the director of the study, said.

We seem to have adjusted to a daily routine that says, "Get teens up before it's light; get them to school by 7:45 ready or not; and let them out by 2:00." To do what?

Even a large proportion of adults have trouble being bright morning people. This goes double for teenagers going through the growth and hormone years.

Since after-school time is such a factor in risky and violent behaviors, maybe we should reorganize high school schedules. When classes begin at 7:45, teens may go home by 2:30 to an empty house, and three hours of unsupervised time before parents get home from work.

Bus drivers and others who have built their schedules around dropping the kids off early would find schedule changes troublesome. Sports practices would be disrupted by a later schedule, and part-time jobs would be more difficult to arrange, but what is our priority? Six dollars an hour or fewer teenage pregnancies? What sense is there in going to math class at 7:45 a.m. in a sleepy haze and going to football practice at your afternoon peak? It should be math at your peak and sports when they can be worked in.

Other studies investigating the sources of school violence show that almost half of all students are concerned about pressure for school grades. The stress builds with the morning rush followed by the cascade of short classes.

If a good education for our kids is our goal, it's time to get started. Let's plan to change their daily schedule to give them the best chance to learn and to practice safe habits.

3. Bullies and Victims

Every school day, 160,000 students will stay home because of bullies, the U. S. Department of Justice estimates. Also, 100,000 students will bring guns to school, 6,500 teachers will be threatened and 250 teachers will be attacked.

Bullies often justify their aggression by saying they were provoked and the victims deserved mistreatment because they didn't comply with the bully's demands. Bullies like to dominate others and think they should always get their way.

Girl bullies may use more subtle tactics than their more violent brothers such as insults and ridicule, but the terror they inflict can still be intense and cruel. So victims avoid unsupervised areas, rest rooms, recreation areas, the lunchroom or Facebook just to keep from being the repeated targets.

Victims of bullies can be passive or provocative. Passive victims are often alone, anxious, sometimes weaker, and may cry easily. Provocative victims can bring trouble on themselves because they tease and irritate others and don't know when to back off. When they get an unwanted reaction, they sometimes fight back, but usually ineffectually.

What can a parent or teacher do? The single most effective deterrent to bullying is an adult authority. We parents and teachers should intervene. We can do it with a no-nonsense style, as a problem solver and as a third person who smooths things over.

In the cafeteria, Taylor, who is 14 and has been the

subject of many bullying complaints, shakes his fist at Richard and says, "You'd better hand over that quarter left over from your lunch."

Ms. Anderson, the social studies teacher, overhears and says, "Taylor, that doesn't go here. Come to my room for the rest of your lunch time—we need to talk." (The no-nonsense and prompt action approach.)

Preventative school policies hold bullies responsible for their behavior. Staff may feel uncomfortable confronting bully behavior and they may ignore it. Or they may feel isolated and unsupported when it comes to intervening in the lunchroom, hallways, or outside of school. The power balance needs to shift—the pendulum needs to swing away from power for bullies and back to the school staff.

"No-Bullying Rules" and school policies that encourage students to speak out and get adult help when needed should be supported by parents. Our goal should be to protect the victims and to help the bully replace negative behaviors with skills that involve treating others kindly.

This problem requires a statement right from the

top. School superintendents should assure principals, and principals should assure teachers that they will be vigorously supported in their efforts to stop bullying in the school and out of school.

One excellent source for help is *Bully-Proofing Your School: A Comprehensive Approach for Elementary Schools,* published by Sopris West, 4093 Specialty Place, Longmont, Colorado, 80504 or, sopriswest.com. This book describes effective long-range programs for schools and parents and it provides useful handouts, exercises, and needed strategies.

The West Middle School of Detroit, Michigan, began its anti-bullying program by displaying school posters with anti-bullying messages such as "Friends aren't friends if they put you down" and "Your silence means your approval." The school also has a "bully box" for students to anonymously report incidents. "No-Bullying Rules" and these school policies encourage students to speak out and to get adult help when needed, and they should be supported by parents of bullies as well as parents of victims. The Detroit program alerts parents to watch their students for telltale habits:

* Making excuses for not wanting to go to school.
* Increased fear of school situations such as riding the bus, going outside or using the rest room.
* Missing personal items or needing extra school supplies or money.
* Extra trips to the school nurse, unexplained bruises or torn clothing.

Until parents take up that awareness, kids will be hiding out in school and losing out on their education while they try to stay out of harm's way. "If I don't go to the bathroom (gym, school bus, outside areas, or lunchroom), I can avoid Billy (or Beth) Bully for another day."

Teachers and principals deserve your support. And many teenagers need special practice learning how to talk firm, walk tall, look a tormentor in the eye and say loudly, "Back off!" As city police often tell us, some people need to practice how to avoid looking and acting like a victim.

Also the bullies need help. They, too, are missing

out on their education while their attention is on confronting, fighting, and abusing.

They will soon be out of school with minimal social skills and the mistaken notion that abusing others is acceptable. They need redirection.

Let's help them now while they are in school and teachers and staff have an influence.

The person who brings the problem to our attention is often denounced as a "tattletale." One reason tattletales annoy us is that the help requested is not easy or comfortable. In some cases, it's dangerous. The bully may retaliate or the bully's parents may object to our interference.

Our freedom and safety exist only because most people will not tolerate behavior that endangers others. If we saw thugs beating up someone, we'd yell for help or call the police. We wouldn't expect the police to say the victim should "solve his own problem." And we would not expect to be ridiculed as a "tattletale."

Bullies at school are a local example of a weakening of the majority's will to protect the individual. Tattletales are not admired and neither are bullies. School polices should encourage students to object when one of their own is bullied by another. And teachers should support reasonable requests for help. Tattletales are not always wrong.

The internet site, CharacterCounts.org, suggests this pledge for schools: "Anti-bully Pledge: We will not bully other students. We will help others who are being bullied by speaking out and getting adult help. We will use extra efforts to include students in activities in our school."

School psychologist Izzy Kalman offers direct help for the kids with a free online manual, *How to Stop Being Teased and Bullied Without Really Trying*. His website, www.bullies2buddies.com also has a free manual and advice for adults.

The rewards for teasing and bullying are in the reactions of the victim, says Kalman. He makes specific suggestions about how a teen should react or not react.

The bullies of today will be the community problems of tomorrow. From their ranks will come the next generation of child abuse, spousal abuse, road rage, and "life rage".

4. Magical Thinking and Mental Habits.

The signers of the Declaration of Independence knew the value of both education and hard work. It was clear to them that effort and learning in school would be rewarded in work and life.

Today, many students believe they might "make it" even to enormous financial success just by luck, or by skill in sports, or by knowing the right people in the entertainment business. It's a possibility promoted by TV, news and state lotteries.

So without incentives to focus attention on the learning at hand, many students become victims of magical thinking about success, and they develop unrealistic views of how "luck" will carry them through.

We adults also become victims of magical thinking. That's why we now approve of lotteries and other gambling, but our grandparents wisely, I think, did not.

We sometimes engage in magical thinking not only about a financial windfall, but also about our students: *"The ones with the 'right stuff' will always do well." "Kids will work harder at school if parents take a harder (more punitive) line or if the teachers enforce strict (more punitive) rules."*

Faced with a student's failure and rebellion, a parent is tempted to criticize and punish. But the solution is on the positive side—with incentives, praise and respect expressed in concrete ways that raise self-esteem and confidence.

Some may object that gushing with praise is the wrong solution, but the danger for most of us isn't in overdoing it, but in doing it at all. Encouragement and parental support involve a commitment of time and attention.

But schools are crowded, teachers are very busy and our culture is inclined to provide little compensation for the essential activities of attending school and learning.

Representatives in Congress with their large salaries and teachers on the line with their modest ones should pause before objecting to the notion of rewarding students. It may be the most important part of the teaching and the parenting job. Few of us work for nothing.

I know it seems like a lot of trouble and we wish all students would work just for the joy of it and learn just for the love of learning, but most will not. We are a goal-oriented species with ambitions that can go astray. We need daily course corrections through positive feedback.

If a student behaves badly in school, we often say it is his fault—he is rebellious, aggressive, too distracted, or not very smart. In a well-known study focused on how we explain children's' problems, school psychologists listed the following causes of school problems:

1. The material was not appropriate,
2. The teacher was not doing a good job of teaching,
3. The organization of the school was wrong,
4. The parents of the student were not supportive,
5. Something about the student was amiss—lack of motivation, low ability, or emotional disturbance.

When teachers were asked to think back about the

students they had taught, they attributed 85 percent of the problems to No. 5, the students themselves. This is partly true, of course, but it attributes the problem to the factor that is most difficult to change.

Both parents and their teens can also engage in the faulty mental habit of blaming a person's basic personality. This can get in the way of resolving the problems. Attention to the daily frequent successes with encouragements and compliments produces the best long-term progress. Knowing the pitfalls of blaming the teen's personality can clear the way to a better attitude and a better solution. Here are a few versions of faulty blaming habits that sometimes afflict both parents and teenagers.

1. Oversimplification.

We are all inclined to simplify to keep order in our mind. Some disorder is inherent, but the habit is destructive.

> "All those teachers are mean."
> "Well, if you would just try a little harder, I'm sure things would get better."

You can see that oversimplification can be both a parent's and a teen's problem. A good step forward in this conversation would be to ask a specific question, *"What would show your teachers your good side?"* Of course, this question won't get a direct and constructive answer, but it will turn the topic toward more productive advice than "trying harder."

2. Absolutes.

We prefer absolutes. Gray areas and contradictions are too hard to handle while an absolute demand seems more likely to get results.

Faced with an absolute demand, *"I want all your homework done before supper, not a bit left or no TV later,"* a teenager may react with his own no-room-for-argument tactic, *"Either you love me or you don't. If you loved me, you would let me do it when I want to, so I guess you don't love me."*

Mom could make better progress here by setting a reachable goal, *"If you have the writing part done before supper, you can do the math after your program."* This suggestion won't stop the arguing, but it is more likely to reach a solution.

3. I'll make them sorry.

> *"I just won't do her stupid project; that will fix her."*
>
> *"Mark, giving up won't hurt your teacher; it will only prolong the problem and it will lower your grade."*

Mark dreams of his power over the teacher, but Mom has to help him be realistic.

4. Everyone is watching me.

> *"My hair looks terrible. And everyone will notice this shirt's crummy and faded."*
>
> *"Lamont, your hair is fine and your shirt is fine, too."*

Mom could do better here by giving Lamont a broader view:

> *"Lamont, what were Althea and Larry wearing last Tuesday?"*
>
> *"Mom, how would I know?"*
>
> *"People don't pay much attention, do they? The same goes for Althea and Larry."*

We all want the best for our children and that's why we are tempted to point out the shortfalls, but it's the example you put in front of them—even the mental habit you show—that has the most impact. A discussion of all sides of the problem will produce the most useful conclusion.

When my daughter, Pam, was 14, she asked if she could go to an older friend's high school party after the next football game. Luckily, I was distracted with yard work at the time and said her mother and I would talk about it. I asked Pam a few questions and heard that most of the kids would be older, but she didn't know much more about it.

Later we found out that her friend's parents would be out of town, and on other occasions they had supplied beer for parties since the kids were too young to buy it themselves.

We said no. Pam complained, said we never let her do anything, promised she wouldn't drink any beer, but we still said no. She made quite a production out of calling her friend and complaining about her old-fashioned parents who said she couldn't go.

Years later she told me that many times she was afraid of some of those "friends" and had hoped we would say no. That way she didn't have to think of herself as a wuss and could blame us for having to back out.

Discipline, Boys, and School Problems - 91

When she later had a 14-year-old of her own who asked if he could have beer at his birthday party, of course she said no. He whined that his friends said they had beer on their birthday. She said that because the argument lasted only a few minutes, she wondered if the strategy from her own teenage years was being repeated by her son.

The struggles between teenagers and parents may not always have clear motives. Even in the mind of the teen, impulses and good intentions may conflict. Sometimes parents have to help by setting down a strict rule.

Whether you are on your own or in a partnership, other parents can create a sounding board for your concerns and provide the assurance that others have problems similar to yours.

A few calls or an announcement in a church newsletter will produce other parents who are willing to take an evening a month for a parent coffee chat.

As their kids reach early teens, some parents are surprised at how much guidance and practice their young teens need. School and friends begin taking up the largest amount of a teen's time and attention and just a little coaching from parents can be a long-lasting help for a teen struggling to adjust to everything at once.

Adults looking back realize that school success was a critical ingredient of happiness in their childhood and teenage years. Comfort and success in school strengthens your teen's self-image and parents' satisfaction. If you can help your teen in this important part of his or her life, what a gift it is! And that success provides more than confidence in academic abilities, it influences feelings of competence and usefulness outside of school as well.

Looking back again, we all remember how we compared ourselves to schoolmates and reached an impression of them and a judgment of ourselves as well—possibly before we were 10, but certainly during our teen years. Parents who have attended their own school reunion after a few years know how the reunion seems to measure us against that old bench mark again. This common reaction to reunions demonstrates how important help in school is to a teenage student.

Greg: *"Mom, I don't want to go to school anymore."*

Mom: *"What? I thought you liked school."*

Greg: *"Well, it's boring and a lot of it doesn't make sense."*

Mom: *"Getting along in school is hard. What part do you do best?"* (Mom shows good listening skills in order to hear the whole story.)

Greg: *"Best? Oh, Math, I guess, but what good is it anyway? And in Geography I just can't remember all that stuff and the kids in there don't like me anyway."*

School is such a large part of a teen's life, and if it isn't going well, it clouds almost all other activities. Greg pointed out several sources of trouble when he said he was bored because he didn't see the use of math, couldn't remember the geography, *and* "the kids don't like me." Let's start with Greg's boredom.

5. Providing Answers to, "Why Should I Do That Stuff?"

Kids who say, *"It's boring"* could be sending a confusing message. They could mean that they have little interest in the subject and they don't see the need, or they could mean they are bored because they can't keep up or, the opposite, they are too far ahead. Parents need to sort out these different meanings before they react.

The poor student who finds school lessons of "no use" usually means he finds no importance *for him* in the tasks that are requested: *"Why should I do that? It's just busy work."* A parent could be misled at this point and start explaining why *she*, the parent, thinks the work is important.

> Mom: *"Math is important, Greg, because one day you'll have to manage your own money and figure out shopping and many other things in life."*
>
> Greg: *"Uh, yeah."*
>
> Mom: *"Also, you need it for the higher math that will get you into college."*
>
> Greg: *"Higher math? There's higher math??? I think I won't go to college."*
>
> Mom: *"Don't talk like that. Of course, you want to go to college."*

The "someday-you'll-need-these-things" approach to this problem is not on target with Greg's original objection. His point was that the work is not important *for him.* Greg's value of the "you'll-need-it-for-college" argument is revealed when he suggests giving up college just to avoid math problems tonight!

Mom needs an approach to the meaningfulness and importance of a good education that is within Greg's short-term view of the world. It won't help to provide more arguments about, *"You can't get anywhere without a good education,"* or, *"Jobs will be harder to get, promotions will be harder to come by, and you'll end up with a hard life!"*

At the moment—in the short run—Greg doesn't want to, or can't, deal with those things. The *"getting anywhere"* idea is too far in the future and too abstract—anyway the people on TV seem to do all right, and some of them don't have much education. And how much education would a person need to earn the amount of money that *Greg* would think is plenty?

So why should Greg study decimals tonight? What use is it to know portions of Geography or American History? Why is spelling important? The answers need to be in the present activities of Greg's life. Remember he's a person with short-term priorities.

As he gains new skills from school each day, he

should be encouraged to use them at home. Sometimes that requires real creativity by a parent. Could Greg use his math to keep track of the family checking account? Receive a fee for doing so? Could Greg handle the grocery list? Take the money and do the shopping? Will he make costly mistakes? Yes. Couldn't he just stay interested in this stuff until he needs it? Probably not.

One mother I worked with showed how such skills are useful by taking her 13-year-old son to the bank with her. She allowed him to go in alone and pay the bills. When he returned with the correct change and explained it all, she gave him a "tip." The "tip" is a parental judgment call and might not be necessary for many boys who would be happy with the importance of the task and trust they were given, but her son will never ask why he has to know decimals —he knows why.

He also bakes for his mother. And when recipes need to be halved or doubled she does not interfere in the calculations. From bitter (and sour) experience he knows the importance of these skills. And he feels a little better about his own worth. He's not *just* a kid, he's a kid with useful skills that his parents respect.

Many skills not covered in school are also important to learn. Cooking, washing clothes, caring for your room, and later on, car care. All tasks present opportunities for teens to learn and gain a feeling of self-esteem as they become competent. The chores may be domestic ones that adults shun or view as burdens, but they still have the potential of letting your teen be productive and helpful *now*.

Parents may need to show great tolerance as they allow practice with these important school-related tasks or tasks of everyday drudgery that parents could do faster. Calm your impatience with the knowledge that just mastering the task is rewarding and insures the further benefit of a little self-pride. Mistakes are easier to tolerate because the benefits of pride and competence form part of their teen's protection against later temptations of self-abuse—drugs and alcohol, for example.

When the task is closer to drudgery than to adventure, more enthusiastic praise will be needed. Ordinarily a person gains very little respect from others for drudgery. Drudgery has little in it to be proud of.

So when a teen asks, *"Why should I do this?"* it may be the beginning of an argument, but it also signals his need for appreciation for doing the job. He's counting on your support for activities that are not very important, fun, or "adult." His question about drudgery is a signal to focus on encouraging him and praising him for a job well done.

Learning must be useful now. Parents should provide experiences that point out, here and now, the usefulness of things learned in school. Certainly even a ten- or twelve-year-old can handle a checking account for the family, or plan and carry out the family food shopping. For school subjects that do not easily apply to daily tasks, parents can influence their teen's respect for the subject by asking questions.

> Mom: *"What was your work in science today?"*
> Greg: *"We named the chambers of the heart and followed a drop of blood through the vessels."*
> Mom: *"I always wanted to know more about that. How does it go through?"*

Show interest in school projects and point out, from news-of-the-day, where knowledge applies.

Parent-teen conversations that bring in schoolwork show the usefulness of Greg's work and improve his respect for himself.

6. Homework Strategies that Work.

Greg's second complaint about school also showed up in Geography. This time it wasn't that he questioned the usefulness of the subject by saying it's "boring," but that he found it "boring" because he was not doing well. This requires parental help beyond showing the topic's usefulness—Greg needs study skills.

Homework that requires staring at materials and memorization can be boring and hard to stick with:

> Greg: *"I just can't keep the states straight. We're supposed to know them by Friday!"*
> Dad: *"What are they going to ask you about them?"*
> Greg: *"We have to point them out on a blank map with no words or anything."*
> Dad: *"Do you have a map?"*
> Greg: *"I have the one in this book. I've been studying it a lot, but I don't remember much."*

> Dad: *"How do you do the "studying" part?"*
> Greg: *"Well, I look at the states and try to remember which ones go where."*
> Dad: *"Greg, I think you need to go through a few drills in a situation like the one you're going to have on Friday. How about tracing that map so we can have one that's blank like the one you'll see on Friday. Then we'll make a few copies when we go shopping."*
> Greg: *"OK. Then I could practice by filling in the names on the copies we make."*

Studying requires practice. Greg has been trying to practice in his mind *("I've been studying it a lot")*, but sitting and staring at a book or homework sheet is not real practice—performance—and Greg has not made much progress.

To make homework time successful, Dad first asks Greg what he is *doing*. Most students who are falling behind don't have a specific target for their effort. When they study, they stare at things—notes or books—they don't DO anything.

Most of us don't have the kind of memory that retains a great deal from just looking; it's the *doing* that will be remembered.

What do you remember from your high school days? Spelling? Math and vocabulary you still use (*do things with*)? But I'll bet you remember very little of social studies, geography, history, or math you never use.

We usually tell our teens to *"work hard"* in school. The "work hard" idea is good advice but by itself, it leaves out the specifics. Successful work shows up in grades if the student is shown how the "work hard" idea is turned into overt practice; not just staring at pages, but reading aloud; not just "trying to remember," but talking to others about the work; drilling important concepts, rewriting notes and important material, and drawing new diagrams or tables that organize facts differently. That's how the idea of "work hard" becomes successful learning.

If you are skeptical of this strategy, try the following experiment:

Pick out a favorite magazine in which there are two articles or stories you have not yet read. Read the first story to yourself in your usual way. Find someone to listen to your report of the story or article and tell them all the detail you can remember —who wrote it, who was in it, what was going on, conclusions reached and so on.

Now go back to the magazine and read the second article or story. This time, stand up and read out loud, with good emphasis and inflection—to the wall if necessary. Now find your listener again and report this story giving all the details you can remember of who, what, and where.

By the end of the second report, I'm sure you will notice how much more you remember of the second story. As one student put it to me, *"Well of course I remember that one, I remember what I <u>said</u>!"*

For the purpose of learning and changing habits there is no substitute for active practice. On your vacation, stare at pages in a novel while lying on the beach if you enjoy it, but if it's for learning, "work hard."

Reading assignments often lead the student to this mistake of leaving out the *doing* part of learning. Many of my students have said, *"I can't believe I did poorly. I went through (stared at) all the material for the test!"*

If you only read it (not really practice) and never use it, it will be gone soon. If reading is the assignment, have your student take reading notes—preferably on cards—for each page. *"Never turn a page without writing something,"* should be the rule.

Give your student the advantage. The reading-note requirement helps in several ways.

1. Notes become a source of motivation because they are a concrete product which can give the student a feeling of accomplishment, right away.

2. Notes are a product that parents can encourage, review, and use as a basis for other rewards, if that's in the plan.

3. The third and most important advantage is that notes provide benchmarks of progress that allow the student to pick up at the right place after an interruption.

It's surprising how much studying is done in small sessions of only a few minutes between interruptions by phone calls, snacks, and chores. Without a note-taking habit, most of us start again at the same place we started before. With past notes, we have a record of where we are and can move on to new material.

4. At review time, the work is condensed as notes, maps, tables, and drill sheets guaranteeing the right material will be memorized. Your student can thereby avoid the misery of thrashing madly through unorganized papers.

A Harvard professor I know has several good guidelines for study time. He always distributes a slip of paper to each student before class. The top line on the slip reads, *"The main point of the day was . . ."* followed by a space for the student to complete the statement. The next line says, *"My question for today is..."* followed by more writing room.

The professor collects the slips each day to see how the main point has been understood and what confusion is in need of more attention during the next class. Students must think, summarize, and question, and the professor has excellent feedback. Many professors now use this procedure.

The most important advice on learning comes from early history when Sophocles said, *"The learning is in the doing of the thing."* When it comes to school work, it's easy for the student to forget how much *practice counts*.

The following guidelines summarize the important points for homework time.

GUIDELINE 1: Use Homework Time in an Active Way!

Action Example 1: Always have pencil and paper handy when reading. Note-taking is good practice, and good practice is good learning. Take notes on every page of reading. Authors and publishers of school books are always struggling to keep the size and expense of books down; nearly every page has something to say. What is it? Write it down.

It's a good idea to put many of these notes in question form. The student should use the headings in the book to make up the questions and use note cards if they are convenient. Note cards encourage review of specifics. As test-time approaches, students with the note-taking habit will already have their own review to study!

Action Example 2: Students should make new lists, drawings and summaries of class materials.

Any new "doing" will help the student remember. Working with other students can produce the same kind of practice and drill. New lists, drawings and charts are more easily remembered by those who create them. I have never had a student fail a course when he produced study notes and other evidence of practice!

Action Example 3: Make up the test. If your students are still concerned about a test, they should construct their own version of the test trying to make it as similar as possible to the one expected. Students often report that more than half of their questions were the same as the ones on the teacher's test! With those questions answered in advance, the students easily remembered their answers and were quickly half way to a good test grade.

Action Example 4: Keep a calendar! The calendar should include plans for homework for each day and a record of successes. It should also include priorities for assignments to study so time is spent on the most important work of the moment.

GUIDELINE 2: Reinforce Practice

Many competing activities have built-in payoffs, but the benefits of studying are often a long way off. Students become more efficient as good study skills develop and the longer they practice good habits the more reliable and useful the skills become. This includes taking study notes, re-doing materials, and keeping a calendar. Future opportunities, grades and preparation for new subjects will have long-range benefits but may be weak motivators for present effort.

So what can a teacher or parent do to reinforce a student who needs to acquire new attitudes and skills to study effectively? While the calendar helps in planning time to study, parents need to help in planning a place to study.

1. Provide a place where active note-taking is convenient. This is just as important to the learning place as freedom from distraction.

2. Talk about subjects your students are taking and create examples of the usefulness of the material.

3. Reinforce knowledge about the subjects by asking questions—even questions that stump parents as well as the student. It might be necessary to look up the answer in the homework materials.

4. Reinforce and praise daily *and weekly grades* that reflect knowledge learned.

GUIDELINE 3: Use a Strategy for Tests

Even after students have acquired good study habits through the guidelines of their own practice and encouragement from parents and teachers, they often complain about having trouble with tests. These test strategies bring positive results in either essay or objective tests.

During objective tests: Certainly every student intends to answer each question, but very often items go unanswered. Two reasons for this are: fear of guessing and failure to remember the question. The student should carefully read *and eliminate* options. Checking off poor choices allows the student to focus on the remaining options and improve chances that small differences will be discovered.

Once an answer is selected, the student should read the first part of the item one more time to be sure that the selection actually answers this particular question. Wrong options are often, in themselves, correct, but not the answer to the initial question.

For Essay Tests: The important guideline here is to answer each question twice—once in outline form and then as an essay answer. A student having trouble with these tests should write a brief outline on another sheet before beginning essay answers.

This first answer can be in the student's own words and shorthand. For example, in response to the question, *"What was important about the Gettysburg Address?"* the student might jot down, *"Lincoln; at graveyard; during Civil War; trying to unite the country; said country must try hard to finish the war; for equality and people to run government; give quote."*

Now, looking at the first answer, the student is likely to complete the second answer in good form. Also, as the student is writing the final answer, new points may come to mind to add to the final answer.

The teacher is more likely to give a high score when the major points are easy to find. And major points will be found more easily if your student's writing is as neat as possible.

If this is a problem, buy an erasable ink pen before the next test!

7. How About a Computer Program to Help Learning?

Computer programs from school or at home can be helpful, especially if the drills are very similar to the other school work and to the tests that evaluate progress. Math and language programs often include useful drills because the content of the drills and the test that comes up later are almost the same.

But for programs in other areas where content can vary, you'll need advice from school about *what* spelling, history, government, or social studies the program should cover.

For most teens, adult encouragements and real life applications are needed to keep interest up. It's the same support from parents and teachers that homework and lessons have always required. Leaving a student on a chair, even one in front of a computer, may not produce learning that shows up on school tests unless parents provide encouragement for practice.

A second limitation of computer effectiveness is in the *action* the student is asked to perform. Remember, learning is in the *doing*. If a student learns to press the right buttons on a keyboard to answer math questions, his performance will be best there and not as good on paper and pencil tests and verbal drills.

It's amazing to us adults that learning 3 plus 5 or the usefulness of 3.1416 on a computer doesn't result in a correct answer on those points on every test paper after that. The student can improve with a computer program, but how the improvement shows up on tests depends partly on how similar the test is to the program, not only in content, but in the *way* the student is asked to provide answers.

Here's another place you can contribute: make up some tests. Arrange to collect information from your teen's school. You need to know the nature and general format of the evaluations they use in the computer subjects you have at home. Then, you can construct practice tests on the computer material, but in the format and style your student will encounter at school. Perhaps *your student* could make up these practice tests for himself and others. Quizzes and drills with pencil and paper will give your teen practice in expressing the answers as required later—when no keyboard is around.

8. An Additional Schoolroom Strategy.

Counselors often coach students to improve their *classroom* habits as well as study habits. Use incentives to encourage your teen to try them also, particularly in classes where your student is "having trouble with the teacher."

1. A student influences a teacher's attitude just as a teacher influences a student's. When there is a choice, your student could sit in a seat as close to the front as possible and keep good eye contact with the teacher during presentations—just as you would practice good listening skills in a private situation.

2. Your student should be alert for a question to ask concerning the material. A continual banter of questions that are unnecessary will do no good, but good questions help learning *and* teaching. Einstein's mother used to ask him when he came home from school, *"Did you ask any good questions today?"* If you try to ask good questions in class, you have reasons to follow the teacher's presentations more closely, and are more likely to learn.

3. Your student should occasionally talk to the teacher about the subject. On at least a weekly basis, he should speak to the teacher about the class with a question or comparison to some aspect of other subjects or experiences.

Some people may object to the contrived nature of these suggestions, but many teens have the mistaken notion that the classroom is, or should be, a place where completely passive learning takes place.

The student needs to know that an active, assertive role is necessary. The fact is that a classroom is a social situation where exchanges are a part of the learning. The exchanges may not influence the teacher's grading, but your teen's relationship with his/her teacher will improve active learning and *that* will improve grades!